SOME ACCOUNT

OF

THE EXERCISES

OF

FRANCIS HOWGILL,

IN HIS SEARCH AFTER

THE SAVING KNOWLEDGE OF GOD:

WRITTEN IN THE YEAR 1655.

TO WHICH IS ADDED

A BRIEF SKETCH OF HIS LIFE.

———

LONDON:

PRINTED BY LUXFORD & CO., RATCLIFF HIGHWAY.

1842.

ADVERTISEMENT.

In making the following selection from the writings of FRANCIS HOWGILL, it has been found necessary, for the sake of perspicuity, to make a few alterations and omissions, but care has been taken to preserve the sense of the original.

The short sketch of his life is principally taken from Sewell's History, Geo. Fox's Journal, and a Memoir of F. H. by James Backhouse.

SOME ACCOUNT, &c.

For the simple's sake, who have erred for lack of true knowledge, (as I did in times past), I shall declare unto you a little in short of my travels in Egypt's land, where darkness is so thick, that if you wait but diligently to see yourselves, you will feel it also.

From twelve years old I set my heart to know that God whom the world professed, and whom I did read of in the scripture, whom Abraham, Noah, Moses and the prophets, and the rest of the fathers worshipped.

And I did fall into the strictest worship that was in that part wherein I lived; and often I desired to be alone, and attended much to reading and meditation ; and then as I was sober and serious alone, I began to see *that all the sports and pastimes, and such as youth delight in naturally, were vanity, and they lasted but for a moment ;* and while I was in folly and wantonness doing of them, the nature which was run into transgression had pleasure in them, but as soon as I came from among them I was judged in myself for what I had done, and it often made me weep. Then I resolved in my will, *that I would never do so again,* and for some time I did refrain from the common practice of those things that I had walked in; but as soon as I came amongst them again, I acted those things again which before I did see to be vanity: but long before that I was checked for many things. And so I walked, often condemned in myself when I was serious, and had no peace, and then not knowing what to do I was in much sorrow when I was alone. I had a desire to be alone, where I might not hear nor see any folly acted, and did not go to the former exercises, although something in me hankered after it; but when I yielded not unto it I was glad, and had peace. And then I began to oppose my fellows, with whom I had walked in wantonness ; and then they began to revile me, and hate me, and scorn me ; yet notwithstanding I mattered not. Then I read much, and prayed in words, often three or four times a day; but I knew not where God was, but in my imagination imagined a God at a distance, and so went on. And I began to grow in knowledge without (which is sensual) and then I was puffed up, for the world admired me, but still I was condemned for vain words and actions, and the root of iniquity grew in me. And then I followed a more strict course, and often went five or six miles to hear some more excellent means, (as they called it), and so did get more words, but still I was the same, nay worse, for knowledge puffed me up. (1 Cor. viii. 1). Then along to about fifteen years of age, I posted up and down after the most excellent sermons, and so became acquainted with all the eminent Christians (so called) in the region where I lived; and I was despised of my parents, and of the world made a wonder, and great reproach came upon me; but still I saw they knew nought, and it was no matter. And so much sorrow fell upon me for four or five years, and when I was turned *within*, I was judged for all my iniquity formerly, and still my heart was showed unto me, that it was corrupt; but as I kept within to the light in my conscience,* I was re-

* As the term Light, and similar expressions used by Friends, are misunderstood by many, an explanatory extract is here given from a cotemporary writer. "And now a word to all amongst you who sit weeping by the rivers of Babylon, and have honest desires after God and his righteousness, whom my bowels yearn over, and sound towards you, that you may not any longer be tossed with the sleights of men, nor feed on their airy notions, which give you not the least strength against sin, but draw out your minds without, to look at Christ at a distance from you, and his appearance in power to come hereafter, though he be near unto every one of you, reproving in the gate or door of your hearts, even as saith the righteousness which is of faith. The Word is near you in your hearts, and in your mouths, the word of faith which we preach (Rom. x. 7 & 8); and this is the same word which was from the beginning preached by the Apostles, and witnessed to be living and abiding for ever, engrafted and able to save the soul. (Jas. i. 21). And this is it which discerns the thoughts and intents of your hearts, and bears witness against every vain thought, idle word, and froward ungodly way, which your own wills, that are not free but bound to vanity, choose. Therefore from your own wisdom, labours, and self-works, which be all wicked, cease; and stand still in the light of this engrafted word (of which the scriptures testify) which is able to save your souls. So may your blind eyes be opened, and you brought into a true sense of your conditions, to see how you have walked in unpleasant places, and that notwithstanding all your knowledge and profession, all is not right in the inward, but corruption still lodgeth in the heart as a partition-wall separating you from God. And to do good of yourselves you have no understanding nor ability, but for ever might have perished in this state, if God in his everlasting love had not given his Son a light

strained from many actions which I had a will to do; and in the instant, when I have been doing any unrighteousness in actions or words, in many things I was often stopped; and when I saw that I did it not a great joy arose in me: and when I had done anything forwardly and rashly I was judged, (Ephes. v. 13) but this the teachers said *was a natural conscience that kept from sin and did restrain it.*

And thus I hearkened to their imagination, and so slighted the Light as too low a thing; that was but common grace that did preserve out of gross evils, but the saints had a peculiar faith and grace. And so I hearkened to them, and still I was convinced of sin (John xvi. 7 & 8); and then they told how *the saints did believe in Christ, and so sin was not imputed, but his righteousness was accounted to them, and so I must seek him in the means, as prayer and receiving the sacrament* (as they called it), and they judged me a worthy communicant; and in great fear I was lest I should eat unworthily, and none could direct me what the body of Christ (1 Cor. xi. 29) was, insomuch that one time I read all the Scripture that spoke of Christ's suffering. And they said, *I must believe he suffered for me:* and I believed all that they call faith, and yet I could not see how he had died for me, and had taken away my sin, for the witness in my conscience told me *I was a servant of sin whilst I committed it* (John, viii. 34); and they told me, *I must not omit that ordinance, for thereby faith was confirmed and strength added.* Insomuch, on the one hand they pressing it as a duty, and on the other hand I saw that the scripture said *he that eats unworthily eats damnation to himself* (1 Cor. xi. 29), I was in fear, notwithstanding none could accuse me without; yet then afterward a great fear fell upon me, and I thought I had sinned against the Holy Ghost (Matth. xii.

---

into the world, to manifest and lead out of this darkness. So in the light (which shows you sin and the inability in self to come out of it) wait, and you will feel in yourselves the sentence of death and condemnation upon the first man which is of the earth, earthy. (1 Cor. xv. 47). And by the operation of God's power, which is manifest in the light, you will feel desires begotten and moving in your souls after righteousness; which motion is the Father's drawing in his love that you may not perish, but come unto Christ, who is the *light and life:* and this is the will of God, who begets by the *word of truth* both *to will and to do* according to his good pleasure." (Phil. ii. 13). — "*A Reproof from the Lord,*" by *John Whitehead,* written in 1656.

31 & 32), and great trouble fell upon me. Then they said, *I had not come prepared*, and yet I had all the preparation that they had spoken of; but still they were physicians of no value.

Then I fasted and prayed, and walked mournfully in sorrow, and thought none was like me, tempted on every hand. So I ran to this man and the other, and they applied promises to me, but it was only words; for the witness of Christ (1 John, v. 10) showed me *that the root of iniquity stood, and the body of sin was whole,* notwithstanding I was kept by a secret power from gross evils; but still sorrow compassed me about, and I questioned all that ever I had, which they said was *grace, repentance and faith.* And then I told them there was guilt in me, and they said *sin was taken away by Christ, but the guilt should still remain while I lived,* and they brought me the saints' condition, who were in the warfare, to confirm it. And so I said in myself, *this was a miserable salvation, that the guilt of sin and condemnation should still stand in me :* and thus I was tossed from mountain to hill, and heard them preach confusion, and so I mattered not for them, and said *sure this is not the ministry of Christ.* And then I ceased long by fits, and did not mind them, but kept still at home and in desert places, solitary in weeping, and every thing that I had done was laid before me, insomuch that every thought was judged; and I was tender, and my heart broken, aud when I could sorrow most I had most peace,* for something spoke within me from the Lord, but I knew him not then. And they said, *it was heresy to look for the word of the Lord to be spoken now in these days, but only in the letter.* And so I regarded it not much, yet often I was made to do many righteous things by the immediate power and word of God, and then peace and joy sprung up in me, and promises were spoken, *that he would teach me himself, and be my God.* (Jer. xxxi. 34, and Heb. viii. 11). And often I did obey contrary to my will, and denied my will, but they told me *this was legal to obey out of fear, and that was slavery ; but there was an evangelical obedience* (as they called it) ; so I got above the fear, and yet acted the former things, which they called ordinances, and they said *that was son-like obedience, and Christ had done all.*

Then there appeared more beauty in those called Indepen-

---

* Was not this the godly sorrow spoken of by Paul ? 2 Cor. vii. 10.

dents, and I loved them, and so joined myself to them, and walked with, and owned them as more separate from the world, and they pressed separation ; but at last I saw it was but in words, that they would do things, and choose officers and members of themselves, and so made themselves an image and fell down to it : yet there was some tenderness in them at the first, but the doctrine was the same with the world's without, of others' conditions.

Then they whom they called Anabaptists appeared to have more glory, and walked more according to the scripture, observing things written without, and I went among them ; and there was something I loved among them : but after they denied all but such that came into their way,.as *out of the fellowship of the saints, and doctrine of Christ, I saw the ground was the same,* and their doctrine out of the life, with the rest of the teachers of the world, and that they had separated themselves and made another likeness.

But still all said, *the letter was the word and rule, and Christ at a distance without us had done all;* and some of them holding free will, others opposing, and all in the will of the creature. And then the doctrine of free grace , (as they called it) some preached, *that all sin was done away, past, present, and to come,* and so preached salvation to the first nature, and to the serpent that bore rule (Rev. xii. 9) ; only believing this, and all is finished. To this I hearkened a little, and so lost my condition within ; but still whithersoever I went this was spoken in me—*his servant thou art to whom thou obeys* (Rom. vi. 16) ; and so being overcome by sin I had no justification witnessed in me, but condemnation.

Then some preached Christ within, but they themselves were without, had but words, and yet they said *all must be within,* (unto which my heart did cleave), and they spoke of redemption and justification, and all within ; and of God appearing in man, and overcoming the power of the devil. And then that in my conscience bore witness (Rom. ii. 15, and ix. 1) that it must be so, and I was exceedingly pressed to wait to find it so, and something breathed after the living God ; and a true love I had to all that walked honestly in what profession soever, and I hated reviling one another, and that they should smite one another, and persecute one another, and with the sufferer I always took part. But still I saw, though they spoke of all things within, that they enjoyed not what they spoke, for the same fruits were brought forth; till at last I saw none walked as the ministers of Christ, and none that pretended to the ministry had any such gift; neither pastor, nor teacher, nor were there any such members as were in the apostles' time.

So at last, having passed up and down, hurried here and there, I saw all the teachers of the world, that they sought themselves, and fed poor people with dead names and deceit, and that they were not the ministers of Christ; and so I saw them all in deceit who did not abide in Christ's doctrine, and so I got myself quit of most of them for ever as I dissented from their judgment, they hated me, and persecuted me.

So at last there was somewhat revealed in me, *that the Lord would teach his people himself* (Jer. xxxi. 34, and Heb. viii. 11); and so I waited, and many things opened in me of a time at hand. And sometimes I would have heard a priest, but when I heard him I was moved by the Lord, and his word in me spoke to oppose, and often as a fire it burned (Jer. xx. 9), and a trembling fell upon me, yet I feared reproach, and so denied the Lord's motion. And it was revealed in me to wait, and I should know his counsel; and the word of the Lord was in me,—*the time was at hand when the dead should hear the voice of the Son of God* (John, v. 25); and it burned in me as a fire, *that the day was near when it should not be, lo! here, nor there, but all his people should be taught of the Lord.* (Isaiah, liv. 13, and John, vi. 45). But still my mind ran out, and out of the fear into carelessness, for the cross of Christ I knew not. And yet I say I was wiser than my teachers I met with in that generation; I do not glory in it, for condemnation is past on it all for ever. Yet still I had ever, as my mind was turned to the light, pure openings and prophecies of things to come, and a belief that I should see the day, and should bear witness to His name; and so when things opened so fast, the wisdom of the flesh caught them. And I went up and down preaching against all the ministry, and also ran out with that which was revealed to myself, and preached up and down the country of the fulness that was in the old bottle, (Matth. ix. 17), and so was wondered after, and admired by many who had waded up and down as myself had; and we fed one another with words, and healed up one another in deceit, and all laid down in sorrow when the day of the Lord was made manifest; for I was overthrown, and the foundation swept away, and all my righteousness and unrighteousness was all judged and weighed, and all was found too light. And immediately, as soon as I heard one declare that the light of Christ in man (John, i. 4, and xiv. 6) was the way to Christ, I believed in the eternal Word of Truth, and that of God in my conscience sealed to it; and so not only I, but many hundreds more, (who thirsted after the Lord, but were betrayed by the wisdom of the serpent), were all seen to be off the foundation, and all mouths were stopped in the dust; and so we stood all as condemned in ourselves, and all saw our nakedness, and were all ashamed, though our glory was great in the world's eye: but all was vanity. But notwithstanding I was ignorant what the first principle of true religion was, yet as I turned my mind within to the light of Jesus Christ, wherewith I was enlightened, (John, i. 9), which formerly had reproved me for all vanity, (Ephes. v. 13), and also as I did own it, it led me into righteousness, and when I turned to it I saw it was the true and faithful witness of Christ Jesus; and then my eyes were opened, and all things were brought to remembrance that ever I had done. And the dreadful power of the Lord fell upon me—with fear and terror—for the sights that I saw with my eyes, and that which I heard with my ears: sorrow and pain. And in the morning I wished it had been evening, and in the evening I wished it had been morning; and I had no rest, but trouble on every side. And all that ever I had done was judged and condemned; and all things were accursed; whether I did eat, or drink, or refrain, I was accursed. Mine eyes were dim with crying, my flesh did fail of fatness, (Psalms, cix. 24), my bones were dried, (Prov. xvii. 22), and my sinews shrank. I became a proverb to all, (Psalms, lxix. 11), yea, to them who had been mine acquaintance, they stood afar off from me. And I sought death in that day, and could not find it; it fled from me. And I sought to cover myself any way (Luke, xxiii. 30), or with anything, but could find nothing. And I would have run any way to have hid myself, but I found nothing but weeping and gnashing of teeth, and sorrow, and terror. I roared out for the disquietness of my heart; I knew not the right hand from the left; I became a perfect fool, and knew nothing, and as a man distracted. All was overturned, and I suffered loss of all in all that ever I did; I saw it was in the accursed nature. And then something in me cried, *just and true is his judgment!* My mouth was stopped—I durst not make mention of his name—I knew not God. And as I bore the indignation of the Lord, something rejoiced; the serpent's head began to be bruised. (Gen. iii. 15). And as I did give up to all his judgments, the captive came forth out of prison (Isaiah, lxi. 1) and rejoiced, and my heart was filled with joy, and I came to see him whom I had pierced (Rev. i. 7) and my heart was broken. And then I saw the cross of Christ, and stood in it, and knew the enmity slain upon it, (Ephes. ii. 16), and the new man was made, and so peace came to be made, (Ephes. ii. 15), and so eternal life was brought in through death (Rev. ii. 10) and judgment. And then the perfect gift I received, which was given from God, and the holy law of God was revealed unto me, and was written in my heart, (Jer. xxxi. 33), and his fear and his word, which did kill, now makes alive. And so it pleased the Father to reveal his Son in me through death (Gal. i. 16); and so I came to witness cleansing by his blood, which is eternal; Glory unto him for ever! and am made a minister of that Word of eternal life which endures for ever; Glory unto his name for ever! and have rest and peace in doing the will of God; and am entered into the true rest, (Heb. iv. 3), and lie down in the fold with the lambs of God, where the sons rejoice together, and the saints keep holy days; Glory unto him for ever!

And these few things have I written for your sakes who walk in darkness, that you may see where you are, and also for you ye high cedars, who trust in the arm of flesh, (Jer. xvii. 5), that you may cease your boasting, and come down from off the pinnacle where you are exalted; for the same must come upon you if ever the Lord you know in truth and righteousness; even through the death of things, in the curse of all knowledge and wisdom, which is from below; yea, through the death of death that rules in you, which must be· slain upon the cross of Christ Jesus, if ever you come to true peace, and witness eternal salvation.

And therefore you diviners and imaginers, who have feigned a faith, and a Christ, and a salvation in your imaginations, and yet think that you may live in the lust and filth of the world, and in the customs and fashions which perish,—I say your expectations shall fail, and you will lie down in sorrow; for where salvation is witnessed the life of Christ is witnessed; but you would have salvation, and the life of the devil brought forth and lived in. But unto all such I say, 'his will be your sentence, *Depart into the lake*. (Rev. xix. 20).

Therefore take warning; for it is not your good words without the life of godliness, nor your swelling speeches, that are accepted with God; for he accepts nothing but what is of himself, and by him wrought in the creature by his own will and power; and this destroys the carnal will, power, and righteousness: and this work, which he worketh of himself, and by his power, and in his covenant, is perfect, (Deut. xxxii. 4), and is accepted of God: and so it is no more the creature, but Christ, who is in all his saints. And here all boasting is excluded, (Rom. iii. 27), for all is of him and from him, that works both the will and the deed, (Phil. ii. 13), and here the Lord is admired in all his works, and his works praise him.

Wherefore all honest-hearted, who travel and are weary, and have found no rest for your souls, I say unto you, Arise! and come away; lie not groveling in the earth; nor seek to know God in your fallen wisdom, (1 Cor. i. 20, and iii. 19), for the well is deep, (John, iv. 11 to 15), and if you know nothing but the old wisdom, which is corrupt and natural, you cannot come to one drop of the living water. Christ is risen, look upward, mind that which draws you from the earth; the covenant of life is made manifest; Glory unto him in the highest! His proclamation is, Ho! every one that thirsteth, come freely and receive of me freely, without money or price (Isaiah, lv. 1) or anything of yours or self. Nay, self must be denied (Matth. xvi. 24) if you would receive of him, that he may be all and you nothing; for he gives freely (Rom. v. 18) and his gift is perfect and pure, without spot, stain, or mixture; and all that receive his gift come by it to be presented perfect to the Father. And this is making manifest to you also, who wait upon him, who is given for a covenant of light (Isaiah, xlii. 6) and peace, and life; and all that receive this gift shall come to hear glad tidings; peace on earth, and good-will to you as you turn to the Light; and this shall be preached in you, by him who is the anointed of God (Isaiah, lxi. 1) and the messenger of the covenant, (Mal. iii. 1), and is sent to preach to the spirits in prison, (1 Peter, iii. 19), and to open the blind eyes, and to set open the prison door (Isaiah, xlii. 7) that the prisoner may come forth to follow and wait upon him, who is the rock of this age, and of all ages; in which all the fathers believed, and were justified, and did eat and drink of this rock; and this rock was and is Christ Jesus, (1 Cor. x. 4), the Light of the world, and who hath enlightened every one that comes into

the world with his true light. (John, i. 9). Therefore I say
unto you who look after righteousness; come hither, you who
are weary, and I will show you where you may have true
everlasting rest, which he hath shed abroad in my heart by
his free grace and everlasting love, made manifest after a long
and dark night, in which I passed without a guide, and so fell
into the pit and stumbled, and then sorrow and trouble compassed me about on every side as an armed man. But now
hath he shed abroad his grace in my heart, which saves me
from sin, (Ephes. ii. 8), and leads out of the works of condemnation into his habitation, where no unclean thing can enter.
(Rev. xxi. 27). And this grace hath separated me from sin,
and hath constrained me to deny myself, and follow him
through the death of the cross, and through the denial of all ;
both country and nation, kindreds, and tongues, and people ;
and from wife and children, and houses and lands, to publish
his name abroad (contrary to my own will) ; and to make
known unto you the riches of his grace, (Ephes. i. 7), which
all who wait in the light of Christ Jesus shall come to see :
and so you may see him whom your souls love and long after,
which have long breathed after refreshment, but none could
speak a word in season to your condition.

Return home again, ye that in your seeking have sought
among the dead, and joined yourselves to strangers, and have
got nothing but a husk, a shadow, and live in a dream. You
are further off in running out, and seeking in your earthly
wisdom and comprehension, than you were before ; and have
got nothing but a report of what Christ said and did, and
how they worshipped him. And so while your eyes have
been without, you never found him, whom the saints and all
that knew him worshipped in spirit, and witnessed him their
salvation in them ; and he was their hope. And the ground
of their hope was manifest in them, (Col. i. 27), and he that
manifested his love in them then, and was their Redeemer,
he changeth not, (Heb. xiii. 8), but is the same to his seed
for ever : and all who wait in the light of Christ, the measure
of God in you, this shall you come to see.

Now therefore, every one that thirsts, come unto Christ
Jesus, who is near you ; and wait to know his word in you,
which is in the heart, (Rom. x. 8) ; for faith comes by the
preaching of it in you, as you diligently wait, and keep your
minds unto it. And this which shows you sin and evil is in
you (John, xvi. 7 & 8) and makes manifest all that you have

acted contrary to it, yea, even all that ever you have done; and it will search your hearts; and is the eye that sees the deceit in all its transformings in you. And it will let you see it hath often checked and called, but you have not answered its call; and so have chosen your own way; and so have gone from the way which is the light of Christ in you; and so run into the broad way. And that which desired after God hath not been nourished, but hath been famished, and another hath been fed, which is now for the slaughter. But now return home to within, to the true light of Jesus, which is that one thing which leads all men that own it to be guided by it. And therefore all you that love the Lord, and wait for the coming of the kingdom of Christ, feed no longer upon imaginations nor vain words; cease from looking lo here and there; for the kingdom of God will the Father reveal in you, (Luke, xvii. 21), as you wait in the measure of the light in you, by which he reveals himself in his sons and daughters, and will bring them to his everlasting fold and true rest. (Heb. iv. 3). All who follow him through the denial of all, and to the losing of all for him, shall come to witness an incorruptible inheritance which never fades away. (1 Peter, i. 4).

Having seen the travail of FRANCIS HOWGILL, in his search after truth, until he attained that which he sought, even "*so to know God as to receive life from him,*" it is thought a few additional particulars might be acceptable to the reader.

HE was born about the year 1618, and resided at Todthorne, near Grayrigg, in Westmoreland. He received a University education, and became a minister in the Episcopalian church, which he left on account of the superstition which he saw remaining in it, and joined the Independents, amongst whom he became a teacher. After this he united himself with the Anabaptists, but without finding that which his soul wanted. He does not appear to have connected himself with any other body of professors until he joined Friends, but, as he expresses it, "went up and down preaching against all the ministry." It was whilst travelling on this errand, in the year 1652, that he met with George Fox, at Sedburg, who on this occasion spoke for several hours, and to whose ministry Francis Howgill bore this testimony,—"This man speaks with authority and not as the Scribes." Though made sensible of the power and authority which accompanied G. F.'s preaching, he does not appear to have been fully convinced of the Truth until the next First-day, for we find him with John Audland on the morning of that day, preaching at Firbank chapel, in Westmoreland. The account of the subsequent proceedings of this memorable day, on which Francis Howgill, John Audland, John Camm, Richard Hubberthorne, and many others, were convinced of the truth, is given in George Fox's words.—" Whilst others were gone to dinner I went to a brook, got a little water, and then came and sat down on the top of a rock, hard by the chapel. In the afternoon the people gathered about me, with several of their preachers. It was judged there were above a thousand people, to whom I declared God's everlasting truth and word of life, freely and largely, for about the space of three hours, directing all to the Spirit of God in themselves; that they might be turned from darkness to light, and believe in it; that they might become children of it, and might be led into all truth, and sensibly understand the words of the prophets, of Christ, and of the apostles; and might all come to know Christ to be their teacher to instruct them, their counsellor to direct them (Isaiah, ix. 6), their shepherd to feed them (1 Peter, ii. 25), their bishop to oversee them, and their prophet to open divine mysteries to them."*

Francis Howgill being on this occasion, as he informs us, convinced " *that the light of Christ in man was the way to Christ*," yielded obedience to its divine teachings, and was soon able to testify, from his own blessed experience, that he is the way—*the only way*—to the Father. (John, xiv. 6). Having witnessed that death unto sin, and new birth unto righteousness, which is indispensable to such a work, the Lord soon sent him forth to declare the truth to others. G. Fox informs us that he " was one of the Lord's worthies that preached his everlasting word of life, from about the year 1652 until the year 1668." The early Friends could in truth say with the apostle,—" we preach not ourselves, but Christ Jesus the Lord," (2 Cor. iv. 5), for the distinguishing feature in their ministry was the endeavour to draw off their hearers from a dependance on man, to a simple reliance on Christ, manifested by his Spirit in the secret of their souls, as their Sanctifier and Comforter, their Counsellor and Guide. And their indefatigable labours were eminently blessed to this end. Having brought men to a living acquaintance with this Divine Teacher, it is very instructive to observe how, *by leaving them to his teaching*, they practically exhibited their belief in the apostolic declaration,—" *But the anointing which ye have received of him abideth in you, and ye need not that any man teach you: but as the same anointing teacheth you of all things, and is truth, and is no lie, and even as it hath taught you ye shall abide in him.*" (1 John, ii. 27). This is illustrated in the case of Francis Howgill. — " The next day (says G. Fox†) we came through the country into Cumberland again, where we had a general meeting of thousands of people, a-top of a hill near Langlands. A glorious and heavenly meeting it was; for the glory of the Lord did shine over all: and there were as many as one could well speak over, the multitude was so great. Their eyes were turned to Christ their teacher; and they came to sit under their own vine, (Micah, iv. 4); insomuch that Francis Howgill, coming afterwards to visit them, found they had no need of words, for they were sitting under their teacher Christ Jesus; in the sense whereof, he sat down amongst them without speaking anything." This remarkable meeting was held in the year 1653, but in the year previously, Francis Howgill suffered his first imprisonment in Appleby jail. In 1654 he came to London, and, in conjunction with Anthony Pearson, held the first Friends' meeting in that city. In the following year, 1655, we find him in Ireland, where, in company with his friend Edward Burrough, he spent about six months, and was finally banished from the country. It was during this visit to Ireland that he wrote the pamphlet from which this tract is taken. It is entitled, "The Inheritance of Jacob discovered," and dated from Cork, the 8th of the 11th month, 1655. From this period to 1661 but little is known concerning him, except that he was at Swarthmore in 1660, and in London in 1661, where he was imprisoned on suspicion of being concerned in the insurrection of the fifth monarchy people. In the year 1662, being a time of hot persecution, he wrote a *very remarkable* paper for the encouragement of his suffering friends.* In the following year, 1663, we find him again in Appleby jail, where he was committed for refusing to take the oath of allegiance. Here he lay until 1664, when he was brought up for trial, and recommitted. "This was in the latter part of the month called March, and he was kept five months† as before, in a bad room, and none suffered

---

* It is given in Sewell's History, vol. ii. p. 18, and is well worth the attention of the reader.

† This five months is the "interval" alluded to in the following remarkable account, which is extracted verbatim from James Backhouse's Memoir. — "It is probable, that it was in the interval between the time of his being recommitted and the following assizes, that the justices indulged him with a few days liberty, to settle his affairs; in the course of which time he felt himself constrained to visit a justice of the name of Duckett, who lived at Grayrigg-hall. He was a great persecutor of Friends, and also one of the magistrates concerned in committing him. Francis Howgill was accompanied by a friend, whose initials were J. D., according to one of the accounts of this visit, of which the editor is in possession of three, which he has received through different channels, all to the same import. By these it appears that the justice was much surprised at seeing Francis, and said to him, — "What is your will now Francis? I thought you had been in Appleby jail." Francis replied to this effect,— "No, I am not; but I am come with a message from the Lord. Thou hast persecuted the Lord's people; but His hand is now against thee, and He will send a blast upon all that thou hast; and thy name shall rot out of the earth; and this thy dwelling shall become desolate, and an habitation for owls and jackdaws." When Francis had delivered this message the justice trembled and said,— "Francis, are you in earnest?" Francis replied,—"Yes, I am in earnest; it is the Word of the Lord to thee: and there are many now living who will see it." This prediction appears to have been remarkably ful-

to speak with him but who got secretly to him without the jailer's knowledge."* At the expiration of the above time he was again brought to trial at the assizes at Appleby, and the following cruel sentence was passed upon him.—"You are put out of the king's protection and the benefit of the law, your lands are confiscated to the king during life, and your goods and chattels for ever, and you to be a prisoner during your life." To which he replied, — "A hard sentence for my obedience to the commands of Christ; the Lord forgive you all." And upon the judge remarking, that if he would be subject to the laws the king would show him mercy; he said,—"The Lord hath showed mercy unto me; and I have done nothing against the king nor government, nor any man; blessed be the Lord! and therein stands my peace; for it is for Christ's sake I suffer, and not for evil doing." And afterwards he signified how contented and glad he was that he had anything to lose for the Lord's precious truth, of which he had publicly borne testimony, and that he was now counted worthy to suffer for it. This cruel sentence was rigorously enforced; and in the year 1668, in Appleby jail, after a sickness of nine days and an imprisonment of about five years, this devoted servant of God laid down his life for the testimony of Jesus. Some of his last words were, — "I have sought the way of the Lord from a child, and lived innocently among men; and if any enquire concerning my latter end, let them know that I die in the faith in which I lived and suffered." After these words he spoke some others in prayer to God; and so sweetly finished his days in peace with the Lord, in the fiftieth year of his age.

---

filled; for according to the testimony of James Wilson,—who was an approved minister amongst Friends, and who lived at one time at Grayrigg Foot, in Westmoreland, and afterwards at Darlington, in the county of Durham,—this justice Duckett had several children, and all his sons died without issue, and some of them came to poverty: James Wilson had also himself repeatedly given alms at his own door to a woman who was the last of the Duckett family. Burns, the historian of Westmoreland and Cumberland, also speaking of this family, in allusion to Anthony Duckett, Esq., and the Grayrigg-hall estate, about the year 1670, says, — "Not long after this, the said Anthony sold the estate to Sir John Lowther, and died without issue; all his brothers also died without issue male; and the name and family, in Westmoreland, is now, 1777, extinct." "Grayrigg-hall, being the ancient manor-house, was a strong old building, in a quadrangular form, adapted more for defence than convenience. It is now, 1777, totally in ruins, most of the lead and timber thereof having been removed to Lowther." Since the time of Burns, the ruins, which "owls and jackdaws" had long inhabited, have been removed, and a farm-house has recently been erected upon the site of the old hall."

* Sewell's History, vol. ii. page 121.

LUXFORD & CO., PRINTERS, 65, RATCLIFF HIGHWAY, LONDON.

Lightning Source UK Ltd.
Milton Keynes UK
UKHW020625051022
409964UK00011B/989